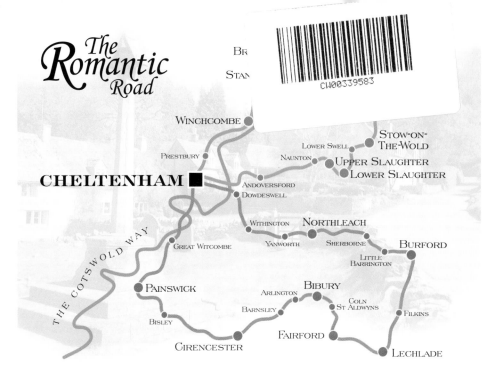

The Romantic Road

BR

STAN

CW00339583

WINCHCOMBE
PRESTBURY
LOWER SWELL
STOW-ON-THE-WOLD
NAUNTON
UPPER SLAUGHTER
LOWER SLAUGHTER
CHELTENHAM ■
ANDOVERSFORD
DOWDESWELL
WITHINGTON NORTHLEACH
GREAT WITCOMBE YANWORTH SHERBORNE BURFORD
LITTLE BARRINGTON
THE COTSWOLD WAY
PAINSWICK ARLINGTON BIBURY
BARNSLEY COLN ST ALDWYNS
BISLEY FILKINS
CIRENCESTER FAIRFORD
LECHLADE

Welcome

Gloucestershire is in my bones. I was born here (in Minchinhampton), spent the most memorable times of my childhood and adolescence here and, fourteen years ago, returned to live here. For good.

I've never set a novel in Gloucestershire, for the very good reason that I wish to continue to live here with a clear conscience! – but I am in no doubt that any writing confidence I have comes from living in a place in which I feel I truly belong.

Of course it's beautiful – nobody who uses this beguiling booklet will be left in any doubt about that. But it's more than just beautiful – it is ancient and interesting and varied and uncompromising. I like that last quality – the fact that the high limestone hills will sustain little but sheep; that winters can isolate the steep valleys; that the winding and often vertical lanes deter all but those who really want to discover and appreciate this remarkable landscape, these memorable towns and villages.

So – off you go, and, as they say on some footpath signs round here, kill nothing but time, take away nothing but memories. And I can promise you that you'll treasure those.

THE COTSWOLDS

In an area so rich in history and natural beauty as the Cotswolds, it is sometimes difficult for visitors – even those who have been before – to get to know the country roads and traditional villages. The Romantic Road aims to provide routes which are easy to follow by car but which also connect with footpaths and cycle routes. They show off the loveliest villages and landscapes, reflecting the romance of their history and literary heritage.

To complete the circular routes at a leisurely pace you would need a full day for each, although you are never far from your starting and finishing point in Cheltenham. Choose from the many places of interest which are described along the way and, for visitors with time, they will offer additional highlights to the scenic journey.

The Cotswolds are a delight all the year round but do remember these charming landscapes can be less hospitable in bad weather. While driving The Romantic Road, be mindful of road and weather conditions on lanes which are sometimes narrow and steep. When cycling or walking, please keep to designated routes and follow the Countryside Code. And finally, please respect the fact that these beautiful towns and villages are people's homes and places of work; indeed, you may well find the true romance of the Cotswolds away from the crowded tourist spots during the busy summer months.

The little roads are warm roads
And fine to house within;
They grow great trees, escape the breeze
And nurse the homely inn;
The high roads are dry roads
For many a thirsty mile;
But their wind and rain I will face again
As I have done many a while.

The little roads are quaint roads
That wander where they will,
They wind their arms round all the farms
And flirt with every hill.
But the high road is my road
And goes where I would go,
Its way it wends as man intends
For it was fashioned so.

JACK HAINES

(1875–1960; Haines enjoyed a reputation as a poet and botanist and frequently took long walks in the Cotswolds with his good friend the celebrated poet and composer Ivor Gurney.)

Lower Slaughter

Lower Swell

The Cotswolds are unarguably romantic. The countryside, from the high, windswept wold down to the tranquil vale that conceals a peaceful village with single pub and ancient church tower, speaks for itself. A country's history is fashioned by great events and its traditions built upon the way people have led their daily lives. Cotswold towns and villages are testament enough to English history. The harmony of the honey-coloured stone and traditional architecture complemented by the natural beauty of the surrounding countryside, is the sweeter side – the romantic side perhaps, of civilisation.

Elkstone

The love of one's homeland is a powerful emotion that may find its expression in words, pictures and music. Cotswold life has engendered an abundance of artistic, literary and musical endeavour and The Romantic Road combines the area's natural beauty with a rich cultural heritage. Here are scenes worthy of Constable, saturated in light worthy of Turner, which have been celebrated in words in every age from Alfred Tennyson and C. Day-Lewis (both residents of Cheltenham) to the eulogising of Shelley, the childhoods of the Mitfords and Laurie Lee and the longings of Ivor Gurney. And around you plays the music of Vaughan Williams and Gustav Holst.

Holst's Birthplace

Holst was born here in Cheltenham, at 4, Clarence Road. He is best remembered for " The Planets". The planet Venus will be your mentor throughout your journey along The Romantic Road.

A ROAD FOR TODAY

The Romantic Road

Your first romantic journey begins at Pittville Pump Room, the epitome of Cheltenham's Regency splendour. Standing under the colonnades, you can readily imagine those visitors some 150 years ago who came to take the waters which were prescribed for a myriad of maladies – from constipation and gout to "scrofulous afflictions, exudation and worms".

Built in the late 1830s by the politician and entrepreneur Joseph Pitt, Pittville Pump Room has since been the venue for recitals and talks, dances and banquets. Today it remains as popular as ever, especially during Cheltenham's International Festival of Music in July. You can still sample the alkaline spa waters, but perhaps you may prefer an invigorating promenade around Pittville Park before embarking upon The Romantic Road.

Pittville Pump Room

Leave Pittville Pump Room and head north on the A435 to the roundabout at Cheltenham Racecourse.

Take the right hand exit signposted to Prestbury, keeping Cheltenham Racecourse to your left.

Cheltenham Racecourse needs no introduction except to state that there has been racing here since 1831. It is the home of the National Hunt Festival in March, featuring the famous Cheltenham Gold Cup.

As you approach Prestbury, follow the signs to Winchcombe along the B4632.

Prestbury is reputed to be one of the most haunted villages in Britain. The most famous of its ghostly residents is the Black Abbott, who roams around the village where he has been known to cause traffic to swerve!

Cheltenham Racecourse

Also well known for its horse-racing connections, the village has been home to many famous jockeys, including Black Tom Oliver and Fred Archer. Fred, who rode a remarkable total of 2,748 winners in his short life, grew up at the Kings Arms in the High Street. There is a plaque which commemorates him. It reads:

At this Prestbury inn lived,
FRED ARCHER the jockey,
who trained upon toast,
Cheltenham water and coffee.
The shoe of this pony
hangs in the bar,
where they drink to his prowess
from near and from far.
But the man in the street
passes by without knowledge
that t'was here Archer
swallowed his earliest porridge.

As we begin to climb up Cleeve Hill out of Prestbury, just beyond the entrance to the Hotel De La Bere, a short detour from the main road to your left brings you to the village of Southam. Take the first turning on the left into Southam Lane. In the village, a signpost to your right directs you to the 12th century church and opposite, the impressive tithe barn. Tithe barns are a common feature of the Cotswolds, linking directly to our medieval past. They were described by William Morris, the great English designer, poet and craftsman, as *"the finest piece of architecture in England, as beautiful as a cathedral"*. The tithe payment was the tenth share of the parish's annual produce, which was taken by the Church to pay the clergy and for poor relief.

Rejoin the B4632 signposted Winchcombe.

Winchcombe

On your way, look out for the little memorial to George Stevens, on your left. He rode in 15 Grand Nationals, winning 5 of them, but he died falling from his horse here in 1871. As you continue the steep climb up Cleeve Hill, it is hard to believe that this road led to a predecessor of the present racecourse, marked now by the three radio masts. The square white house on the right, half way up the hill, was the home of Doctor Bronowski, whose television series, "The Ascent of Man" was popular some years ago. Immediately after Stockwell Lane is a viewing point where you can stop and enjoy a wonderful view across the Severn Vale. The panorama continues from the Severn Bridge to your left, sweeping across the Black Mountains, to the splendour of Tewkesbury Abbey and the Malvern Hills to your right.

Continue over Cleeve Hill and down into Winchcombe.

The ancient Saxon borough of Winchcombe today offers the passing visitor little clue to its former importance. It is worthwhile travellers on The Romantic Road stopping here and exploring on foot. *"There is scarcely a place in England held in greater respect, or where more pilgrims attend"* said the 12th century chronicler William of Malmesbury. Its Benedictine Abbey, with its shrine to the boy Saint Kenelm, was built by King Kenelf of Mercia in 811 and was a major site of pilgrimage in Medieval England. Today, the little town is dominated by the majestic wool church of St. Peter's. Look out for the grotesque carvings on the parapets. Some are demons and some are caricatures of local dignitaries. Look out for the mad hatter and the helmeted knight with stomach ache!

In the 17th century, the area around the town was famous for its tobacco crop. All that remains today to remind us of this period is the street name "Tobacco Close". Whilst exploring, look out for the seven-holed stocks outside the town hall and the tiny house, reputed to be the smallest in Gloucestershire, tucked away on the right hand side of the main street. On the outskirts of Winchcombe is Sudeley Castle – once the home of Katherine Parr, the last wife of King Henry VIII and the only one to survive him. She is buried at Sudeley, thus betraying the King's dying wish that they should lie together for eternity in the Royal Vault at Windsor. Within one year of Henry's death, Katherine had married Sir Thomas Seymour and they had made the Castle their home. Sudeley Castle is also immortalised as Blandings Castle in the novels of P G Wodehouse, who when visiting Cheltenham, liked to walk across Cleeve Common and look down at the Castle in the vale beneath:

Sudeley Castle

"The morning sunshine descended like an amber shower-bath on Blandings Castle, lighting up with a heartening glow its ivied walls, its rolling parks, its gardens, outhouses…green lawns and wide terraces, noble trees and bright flowerbeds."

Hailes Abbey

Sudeley Castle welcomes visitors travelling The Romantic Road. The splendid gardens feature among its many attractions.

Leave Winchcombe continuing along the B4632 following signs to Stratford and Broadway.

Just outside Winchcombe is Hailes Abbey, once famed for housing a Relic of Holy Blood, rashly certified as genuine by Pope Urban IV. The Abbey was founded in 1246 by the brother of Henry III who had vowed this deed after surviving a shipwreck on his return from crusading in the Holy Land. It was destroyed by Henry VIII during the dissolution of the monasteries in the 16th century. The abbey is open to visitors. Trees have been planted to show the plan of the abbey where walls no longer remain.

Continue along the B4632 for another mile until you reach a roundabout. Take the right turn signposted Stow along the B4077.

Gloucestershire and Warwickshire Railway

Immediately on your right is the entrance to the GWR – not the Great Western Railway, or even God's Wonderful Railway, but the Gloucestershire and Warwickshire Railway! Here the traveller can step back in time to experience the romance of the steam age. The preserved railway line offers a thirteen-mile round trip on trains hauled by historic steam locomotives.

After approximately three quarters of a mile take the left turn signposted to Stanway and Stanton.

At the junction notice the beautiful George and Dragon memorial to the men of Stanway lost in the Great War. As you descend the hill, the magnificent Jacobean Gate House to Stanway House *(pictured below)* comes into view, and as you turn the bend in the road you are greeted

Stanton

with the sight of the neighbouring church. Romantic and beautiful Stanway House dates from the 16th century when the Tracy family acquired the manor on the dissolution of Tewkesbury Abbey. So, there has been a change of ownership only once in the last 1270 years. There is a 14th century tithe barn, now used as a meeting hall, a splendid eye-catching pyramid of 1750 on the hillside . . . and a dog cemetery for the much loved family pets of successive generations. Stanway House was also the location for the filming of Edith Wharton's "The Buccaneers". The house and its spectacular gardens can sometimes be visited on summer afternoons.

The Romantic Road

The village of Stanway was once the home of Thomas Dover. Dover made his fortune as a privateer but in the best traditions of a romantic adventurer, he is remembered for rescuing the real-life Robinson Crusoe – Alexander Selkirk – from his unscheduled and extended stay on a desert island. As we follow the road around the church, look out on the left for the village cricket field. The thatched roofed pavilion is known locally as Pan's Pavilion, the gift of J M Barrie, creator of Peter Pan, a frequent visitor to Stanway and a keen cricketer.

Continue along the road out of Stanway for approximately one mile. At the next road junction, take the right fork signposted to Stanton.

Stanton

Picturesque Stanton is best explored on foot. Many of the buildings date from the 16th and 17th centuries, being lovingly restored in the 20th by the architect, Sir Philip Stott, who bought the estate in 1906. The village church of St. Michael and All Angels contains 15th century stained glass from Hailes Abbey and fine woodwork of the 20th century. The traveller can take refreshment at the appropriately named "Mount" inn.

Broadway

Leaving Stanton, take the road signposted Broadway and rejoin the B4632, turning right signposted to Stratford.

At the next T junction, turn right into Broadway, one of the most famous of all Cotswold villages. Then take the first turning on the right, signposted to Snowshill.

If you wish to explore Broadway, park your car in the public car park on your left, in Church Close. One of the best loved of all Cotswold villages, Broadway's popularity is long-lived. It developed as a staging post on the route between Oxford and Worcester, where coaches and horses could rest at the Lygon Arms before the long pull up Fish Hill. Both King Charles I and Oliver Cromwell are reputed to have patronised the Lygon Arms.

It was William Morris, in the 19th century, who set the romantic tone to the town, imploring other writers and artists like Henry James and Rosetti to visit with him. John Singer Sargent painted his famous work "Carnation, Lily, Lily, Rose" in the garden of Farnham House. Gordon Russell, the fine furniture maker, established his workshops in Broadway. His father owned the Lygon Arms.

Continue out of Broadway up the hill towards Snowshill. At the top of the hill, after 2¹/₂ miles, the entrance to Snowshill Manor is on your right.

A Tudor house now in the care of the National Trust, it is Snowshill Manor's more recent history that holds its romance. Charles Paget Wade, as a soldier in First World War France, saw a picture of Snowshill Manor in a copy of "Country Life" magazine. Struck by its beauty and tranquillity, he determined to one day live there and survived the war to return and buy the property in 1919. A wealthy eccentric who inherited a fortune from the family sugar plantation in St. Kitts, in the West Indies, Wade began to fill the house with a plethora of antiques, artefacts and memorabilia. His collection became so vast that he moved out and lived in the adjacent and very spartan Priest's House!

Snowshill

Bearing right at the fork in the road, carry straight on into Snowshill Village and take the left turn immediately past the church.

Climbing out of Snowshill, go straight ahead at the crossroads signposted to Broadway Tower and Chipping Campden. Take the first left turn and then follow the brown tourist signs for Broadway Tower, passing the Tower and Country Park on your left.

Broadway Tower

Built on an ancient beacon site, The Tower is a fine example of a folly, built in 1797 by the Earl of Coventry as a gift to his wife – from it, she could see her family's home at Croome Court in Worcestershire. Needless to say, on a clear day, it commands magnificent views over the surrounding countryside. The Tower was constructed with 74 steps and a room on each floor. Towards the end of the last century, William Morris spent a memorable summer holiday at the Tower with a group of Pre-Raphaelite artist friends. This visit is commemorated by an exhibition of Morris's works. Broadway Tower and Country Park are open to visitors.

Cross the A44 signposted to Saintbury and follow signs for the village, taking the first left turn. The road then bends immediately to the right passing the Dormy House Hotel and Broadway Golf Club.

Passing down the hill through Saintbury, rejoin the B4632 turning right signposted to Stratford.

Follow the road into Weston Subedge.

Sheltering beneath the limestone "edge" or escarpment of the Cotswolds, Weston straddles Ryknield Street, the ancient Roman road which runs between Stow-on-the-Wold and Alcester in Warwickshire. Signposted in the centre of the village, a small detour brings you to Dover's Hill. This was the panoramic venue for the Cotswold Olympicks initiated by Robert Dover in 1612. Dover used his connections at Court to win permission from King James I to hold the Games which included such events as shin kicking and jumping in bags! Banned by the local vicar in 1851 because of hooliganism, the games were revived one hundred years later but "progress" had changed them into a shadow of their former incarnation when up to 30,000 people would throng the hillside.

Continuing through Weston and out of the village, at the next road junction turn right onto the B4035 signposted to Chipping Campden.

Passing through Aston Subedge, continue on towards Chipping Campden. There is a sign to Hidcote on the left.

For garden lovers our romantic journey offers the opportunity to visit two of the most beautiful gardens of the Cotswolds. Hidcote Manor Garden, now in the care of the National Trust, is probably the most celebrated of all Cotswold gardens. They were created by Major Lawrence Johnston, a disciple of Vita Sackville-West. After returning from The Boer War, he undertook the restoration of the Hidcote estate which his mother had bought for him as a project. The result is a wondrous series of outdoor "rooms" each with collections from Johnston's travels in Mexico, South Africa and China.

Hidcote Manor Garden

Close by is Kiftsgate, famous for the 50ft climbing Kiftsgate Rose. Begun after the First World War, the gardens offer dramatic views over the Cotswold escarpment. Kiftsgate shared in the bounty of Lawrence Johnson's travels, witnessed by the collection of tree peonies brought back from China and Japan.

We now enter the historic Cotswold town of Chipping Campden.

The first notable Lord of the Manor of Chipping Campden was Earl Harold, whose fate at the Battle of Hastings in 1066 is announced in every English history book. It was probably Sir Baptist Hicks, Lord of the Manor during the reign of Charles I, who put Chipping Campden on the map. Making a fortune as a silk and cloth merchant, Hicks was so wealthy that he lent money to the King, as well as building the market hall and almshouses and his own lavish home next to the church. Unfortunately, only the gatehouse and banqueting houses remain after the main house was burnt to the ground during the ensuing Civil War. Hicks and his family now rest in splendid tombs within the church.

Chipping Campden

It was the steward to Hicks' daughter who was the central figure in a bizarre incident: seventy year old William Harrison inexplicably disappeared in 1660, three people being accused of his murder and hanged on Broadway Hill. Two years later he returned safe and well! Nobody has found out the truth behind "The Campden Wonder." Inspired by William Morris's Arts and Crafts Movement, CR Ashbee formed an artists' community in Chipping Campden after Morris's death, moving the influential Guild of Handicrafts out from London's Whitechapel. From 1902 to 1911, Ashbee made his home in the Woolstaplers Hall. The Old Silk Mill in Sheep Street still houses craft workshops.

In the town centre, turn left into Sheep Street signposted to Bourton-on-the-Hill. Take the next left turn signposted to Broad Campden and Blockley.

In the garden of the Quaker Meeting House in Broad Campden is the unmarked resting place of Jonathan Hulls, an 18th century clock repairer. One of history's tragic failures, who was later proved to have been a genius, Hulls came up with the radical idea of powering boats by steam power. His trials on the River Avon at Evesham ended in abject failure, however, and public ridicule led him to abandon his idea. His portrait later hung in the state room of the Queen Mary! Hulls' genius subsequently showed itself in other ways, and his legacy to mankind was the invention of the slide-rule, the precursor of the calculator.

Broad Campden

Leaving Broad Campden, turn right signposted to Blockley and Moreton-in-Marsh. Heading up the hill, you can rest a moment on the roadside bench and look back into the valley.

Blockley was once a thriving "industrial" village supplying silk thread to the Coventry ribbon-making trade. By 1850, there were 6 mills employing some 600 people. In 1887, the same water power was used to light up the village – with Blockley becoming the first village in Britain to have electricity.

The village was famed as the refuge of the 19th century prophetess Joanna Southcott. She moved to Rock Cottage in 1804 and died in

Blockley

1814, leaving behind a sealed box alleged to contain the secret of world peace and predictions for the future. Her instructions were that it was only to be opened in the presence of 24 Bishops of the Church of England. The box was x-rayed and found to contain a cocked pistol! Another box, allegedly hers, was opened in 1927 and found to contain a lottery ticket and a night cap! Her followers in the English Panacea Society still maintain that the real box has yet to be opened and regularly advertise for the Bishops or their representatives to do so. Rock Cottage was tragically gutted by fire in 1971, destroying many of her "Communications". It has since been restored. Blockley was more recently the home of Doris Lindner who created the bronze statue of champion hurdler Arkle, now displayed at Cheltenham Racecourse. On summer days, Mill Dene Garden, a Cotswold water-mill garden set near the centre of the village, is open to visitors.

Arriving in Blockley, turn left following the sign to Bourton-on-the-Hill, then turn right at the next junction into Lower Street. This road will take you out of the village.

Now head south along the B4479 towards the A44, passing signs for Batsford on your left.

Turn left onto the A44, signposted Moreton-in-Marsh and Oxford, passing down through the village of Bourton-on-the-Hill.

Blockley

Beyond the village, on your left, you will pass the entrance to Batsford Arboretum. Batsford Arboretum was planted by the first Lord Redesdale, ambassador to Japan during the 1850s. Bucking the Victorian trend, he created a "wild" garden with over 1000 species of trees, noticeably magnolias and maples, as well as a Japanese garden and oriental sculptures. The gardens can be visited and provide a colourful diversion on The Romantic Road. Lord Redesdale was also the grandfather of the "Mitford Girls" – Nancy, Pamela, Diana, Unity, Jessica and Deborah. From their childhood home at Batsford Park, the celebrated siblings defined the eccentricities of the 1930s upper classes, some achieving infamy for championing British Fascism.

Opposite, on your right, is the entrance to another celebrated Cotswold house and garden which welcomes visitors, Sezincote. The famous Brighton Pavilion was created following a visit by the Prince Regent to Sezincote in 1807 where he was inspired by the Nabob's house, a moghul-style house which was set amongst the oriental water gardens created by Sir Charles Cockerell at Sezincote.

John Betjeman's "Summoned by Bells" tells how . . .

Moreton-in-Marsh

We'd drive to Sunday lunch at Sezincote
First steps in learning how to be a guest
First wood-smoke-scented luxury of life
In the large ambience of a country house . . . exotic Sezincote!
Stately and strange it stood, the Nabob's house
Indian without and coolest Greek within . . .

Head on into Moreton-in-Marsh. At the junction with the A429 turn right, signposted to Cirencester.

To explore Moreton-in-Marsh, turn left at the junction with the A429, and park in the main street (except on Tuesdays when the town's busy market is held here). The Curfew Bell on the tower at the corner of Oxford Street is a noted local landmark, and was rung daily from 1633 to 1860.

Moreton-in-Marsh

Continue along the A429 for 4 miles towards Stow-on-the-Wold. This road is also known as the Fosse Way, an ancient Roman Road which ran from Exeter, through Cirencester, across the Cotswolds and on to Leicester and Lincoln.

"All roads lead to Stow". To visit, turn left at the second set of traffic lights and enter the town square.

Stow-on-the-Wold
Where the wind blows cold
And the cooks can't roast their dinner!

Both a major coaching stop and sheep town, this is the highest town in the North Cotswolds and is built around its enclosed market square to protect it from the elements. Daniel Defoe wrote that more than 20,000 sheep were sold in one day in Stow-on-the-Wold, a town more likely now to be thronged with visitors than with sheep, though there are still twice-yearly horse fairs. The last great battle of the first English Civil War was fought here in 1646. The Royalists under Sir Jacob Astley were overwhelmed by the Cromwellian army, and many were imprisoned in Stow church. "The blood ran down Digbeth Street". The Royalist Hotel is the oldest Inn in England, recorded in the Guinness Book of Records.

Stow-on-the-Wold

From Stow-on-the-Wold turn right off the A429 at the third set of traffic lights signposted along the B4068 to Lower Swell and Naunton.

The charming villages of Upper and Lower Swell may take their name from the nearby Lady's Well.

Left above: Upper Swell
Above: Upper Slaughter

Passing the crossroads on the green in Lower Swell, take the left turn signposted to The Slaughters. Drive on into the village of Lower Slaughter.

Turn right over the bridge and follow the signs to Upper Slaughter, following the river on your right.

"The Slaughters" are very popular Cotswold beauty spots, typifying the rural idyll of Cotswold villages. During the quieter months of the year it is rewarding to park in one and walk to the other. If you have time, stroll along the river bank in Lower Slaughter to the Old Mill Shop and Museum. Upper Slaughter is the setting for the "Diary of a Cotswold Parson". The parson in question was Francis Edward Witts who served the parish between 1820 and 1852. At some point during this time he assumed the title Lord of the Manor, and his former Rectory is now the celebrated "Lords of the Manor" Hotel and Restaurant. It was a previous Lord of the Manor in the 12th century who perhaps gave his name to the villages: de Soletres.

Bourton-on-the-Water

Climbing out of Lower Slaughter, follow signs to Cheltenham, eventually reaching the junction with the B4068.

Take the left turn signposted to Cheltenham. After approximately a mile, take the right turn into Naunton.

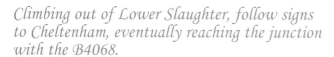

Naunton is the last of the Cotswold villages you will be visiting on your romantic journey. A look round Naunton reveals a dovecote of typical Cotswold design, dating back to 1600. With its 1176 holes, it is reputed to be the largest in England. Naunton church still displays the Table of Kindred and Affinity which acts as a genealogical chart, expounding at great length the family members whom a man or a woman were forbidden to marry.

Continue through Naunton village and climb back up to the B4068, turning right to Cheltenham.

The countryside you are now crossing was once common land, as eloquently described in William Cobbett's "Rural Rides" in the 1820s. When the Enclosures Act dictated the parcelling up of this open land, there was no

Naunton

ready supply of wood to fence in the fields, and the soil was too poor to cultivate hedgerows. It was these circumstances which gave birth to the drystone walls which today are such an integral part of the Cotswold landscape.

Reaching the A436, turn right signposted to Cheltenham.

Many villages throughout the Cotswolds did not survive the thin margin between life and death on the exposed uplands. Their populations dwindled and disappeared through a combination of poor harvests, increased taxation and finally, in 1348/9, the Black Death. The demise of Harford was more violent, however, destroyed by the Knights Templar to make way for their sheep runs which funded their Preceptory at Temple Guiting.

Cheltenham

We are now at the end of our Romantic journey for today. To return to Cheltenham follow the A436 for approximately 3 ¹/₂ miles to the traffic lights at the junction with the A40. Turn right at the lights and follow the A40 through Charlton Kings back towards Cheltenham town centre.

The Romantic Road

Travelling The Romantic Road?

Complete our questionnaire and you could win a romantic break for two.

We need your help to ensure that *The Romantic Road* continues to meet the expectations and needs of visitors seeking to experience the best of Cheltenham Spa and the Cotswolds. Our policy is to keep The Romantic Road under constant review, to improve it at every opportunity and to ensure that it is kept up-to-date and enjoyable. By answering the following questions and returning the completed form, you will provide us with valuable information to help us to achieve these aims. Feel free to leave blank any questions which you would rather not answer. Completion of the questionnaire should not take more than a few minutes. Your name and address will not be stored on a computer database or used for direct mail purposes.

Every six months, all returned questionnaires will be entered into a prize draw with the winner receiving a FREE romantic break for two in Cheltenham Spa (travel not included).

Thank you for your help
Cheltenham Tourism

ABOUT THE ROMANTIC ROAD

1 Which *Romantic Road* have you travelled?

A ROAD FOR TODAY   All ▣   Part ▣   None ▣

A ROAD FOR TOMORROW   All ▣   Part ▣   None ▣

(please tick the appropriate answers)

2 How long have you spent travelling *The Romantic Road*?

1 day ▣   2 days ▣   3 days ▣   more ____ *(please state)*

3 How would you rate the routes you have travelled?

Award marks on a scale of 1 to 6, with 1 being the lowest score and 6 being the highest. Please circle your scores.

A ROAD FOR TODAY	*Lowest*				*Highest*	
Route Instructions	1	2	3	4	5	6
Readability	1	2	3	4	5	6
Tour Content	1	2	3	4	5	6
Overall enjoyment	1	2	3	4	5	6

A ROAD FOR TOMORROW	*Lowest*				*Highest*	
Route Instructions	1	2	3	4	5	6
Readability	1	2	3	4	5	6
Tour Content	1	2	3	4	5	6
Overall enjoyment	1	2	3	4	5	6

4 If you have not been able to travel the whole of *The Romantic Road*, do you have any plans to return to complete your journey?

Yes ▣   No ▣   *Please give details of your future intentions if known:* _____

_____

5 Have you visited any of the attractions, gardens etc. featured along *The Romantic Road*?

Yes ▣   No ▣   *If yes, please write their names:* _____

_____

6 Would you recommend *The Romantic Road* to friends?

Yes ▣   No ▣   *If no, please give reasons:* _____

_____

_____

7 From your experience, are there any corrections or changes required to keep *The Romantic Road* up-to-date?

_____

_____

_____

8   How could we improve *The Romantic Road*?
_____

_____

_____

9   How did you learn about *The Romantic Road*?
    (please tick any that apply)
    Recommended by friend
    Review in Newspaper / Magazine
    Advertisement
    Promotional Leaflet
    Holiday / Travel Exhibition
    In Tourist Information Centre
    Purchased Guide in Book Shop
    Other (please state): _____

ABOUT YOUR VISIT

10 At what time of year did you travel *The Romantic Road*?
    J   F   M   A   M   J   J   A   S   O   N   D
    please circle the appropriate month(s)

11 How many people in your holiday group, including yourself,
    were in the following age groups?
    0 to 15   16 to 24   25 to 34   35 to 44
    45 to 54   55 to 64   Over 65 years

12 Did *The Romantic Road* influence your decision to visit Cheltenham?
    Yes   No

13 How long did you stay in Cheltenham?
    Day visit   1 night   2 to 3 nights
    4 to 7 nights   Over 7 nights

14 Did your decision to travel *The Romantic Road* cause you to extend
    your stay in Cheltenham?
    Yes   No   If yes, by how much?
    1 day   2 days   3 days   more _____ *(please state)*

15 What type of accommodation did you use?
    Hotel
    Guest House / B&B
    With friends and relatives
    Caravan / Camping
    Self Catering
    Other (please specify) _____

The **Romantic** *Road*

16 What was the main purpose of your visit?

Shopping

Special event / Festival / Race meeting

Conference / Meeting

Visiting friends and relatives

Touring Britain

Short Break

Touring Cheltenham and the Cotswolds

Travel *The Romantic Road*

ABOUT YOU

17 Approximately how many miles from Cheltenham do you live?

0 to 50   50 to 100   100 to 150

150 to 200   200 or more

18 If you are visiting Britain, which Country are you from?

_____

19 Which national newspapers and magazines do you read regularly?

National Daily

National Sunday

Local Newspaper

Magazines

Thank you for your assistance. To enter for our FREE PRIZE DRAW, please add your name and address.

Name

Address

Postcode

Would you like to receive a copy of the current Cheltenham Visitor Guide? Yes   No

Please return your completed questionnaire to:
Cheltenham Tourism, FREEPOST CM32, Cheltenham GL50 1PP
(no stamp required if posted in the United Kingdom)

To enter the FREE PRIZE DRAWS the last date for receipt of completed questionnaires is 31st March 2001

CHELTENHAM
BOROUGH COUNCIL

CHELTENHAM SPA
Centre for the COTSWOLDS

4/99/30K

A ROAD FOR TOMORROW

For your second Romantic journey, take the A40 eastbound from Cheltenham along London Road, in the direction of Oxford.

Less than two miles from the centre of Cheltenham, you will pass through the outskirts of Charlton Kings, an old farming community. The village proper has many literary connections – the popular Victorian poet Sydney Dobell lived here. "Alice through the Looking Glass" possibly originated in a visit the real Alice paid to her grandfather, the Rev. George Liddell in Charlton Kings. Lewis Carroll came to see her there and the famous looking glass is still in the house. The real Tailor of Gloucester is buried in the Charlton Kings cemetery, but his true story is not as colourful as told by Beatrix Potter.

Beyond Charlton Kings, the A40 rises into the open countryside of the Cotswolds. Just after the inn on the right, you will see the waters of Dowdeswell Reservoir on the left. At appropriate times of the year, you may notice a curious road sign depicting a toad. The A40 bisects a regular migratory route from the reservoir and drivers are asked to pay special attention to avoid this endangered species.

Take the first road on the right after the reservoir, signposted to Dowdeswell.

The road climbs steeply, passing a Tudor farmhouse and the parish church with its small stone spire.

Go straight across at three sets of crossroads and follow the signs for Withington.

The tower of Withington church will soon provide a good directional landmark. Withington has a wonderful backdrop of woods and is situated near the head of the picturesque Coln valley.

On entering the village, continue past the church and its belt of ancient yew trees and follow the sign for the Roman Villa (and Compton Abdale).

Dipping down into the valley, you may be tempted by the Mill Inn, through whose garden runs the River Coln.

Shortly after the car park of the Mill Inn, you will be turning sharp right, signposted towards the Roman Villa and Yanworth, passing the village's second public house, the King's Head. Keep following the signs for the Roman Villa and Yanworth.

The Romantic Road now takes you through some of the most beautiful valleys, woodland and farmsteads in the Cotswolds. Eventually, the road to the Roman Villa will lead off to the right whilst you will continue towards Yanworth and Northleach. At various times of the year, teas, coffees and homemade cakes are served in Yanworth Village Hall. You may notice the churchyard gate made of horseshoes and the one-handed clock on the church tower.

THE ROMAN VILLA

"Scratch Gloucestershire and you will find Rome". The Romans certainly had good taste when they chose this site in the Coln Valley for their exquisite villa, which dates from AD 120. It was discovered by accident in 1864 when a gamekeeper, who was digging to retrieve a lost ferret, came across a mosaic pavement. Cared for by the National Trust, the remains are some of the best preserved in the country. A visit here is an opportunity to ruminate on the passing of even the greatest of civilisations. The poet, Jim Turner wrote the following lines with regard to the Roman occupation of the Cotswolds:

The Roman Villa

"Did Tribune or Centurion
Find solace in a British home
Where colder Cotswold rivers runs
Far from the Tiber, far from Rome?"

Northleach

At a minor crossroads, go straight ahead following signs to Northleach and Stow-on-the-Wold.

The road to Northleach quickly brings you to a junction with the A429, where you should turn left and travel for a short distance towards Stow, before coming to a set of traffic lights, where you turn right for Northleach town centre.

At this crossing on the old Roman Fosse Way is the excellent Cotswold Heritage Centre. Formerly a House of Correction, a pioneering prison of 1789, it is now a museum of rural life. It also houses a small

Tourist Information Centre. You enter Northleach along the West End and will come to the main square on the right, where there are parking spaces and public conveniences. In the Middle Ages, Northleach was one of the most important wool trading centres and the town is still dominated by the magnificent "wool church" of St. Peter and St. Paul. A unique attraction based at Oak House on the High Street is Keith Harding's World of Mechanical Music.

The Romantic Road waltzes along the High Street past the Union and Red Lion pubs and takes the first left immediately after Keith Harding's World of Mechanical Music towards Farmington. At the next T-junction, you turn right into Farmington and pass the little green en route for the Sherborne and Windrush valleys.

Sherborne is typical of many Cotswold villages which you will encounter. Each has its own characteristics, though all have features in common. All have their church; most have a pub; and many have a Manor, or a Hall or grand House. You will pass, on the right, Sherborne House, said to be haunted by a previous owner, the hunchback royalist, Crump Dutton. Next, the village church, on a rise overlooking Sherborne Brook, where centuries ago, thousands of sheep would have been seen grazing. Here is a simple stone bridge where stately swans may be seen. Sherborne was the birthplace of James Bradley, a 17th century Astronomer Royal who was first to calculate the positions of the stars. Continue through the village, noting the rows of Victorian cottages on the left. One is a Post Office and shop of some charm. The last cottage, no. 88, boasts a Norman front door.

Sherborne

Follow the road as it bears round towards Windrush and the Windrush Valley.

The Windrush is "a laughing little river where it runs between the hills". Its romantic name is derived from the Anglo-Saxon "wen" (wind or meander) and "risc" (rush, or river grass), especially apt as you listen to the breeze rushing through the reeds. The next village is Windrush itself – drive through keeping to the main road, with the village green on your right. Local stone and local craftsmen were employed by Sir Christopher Wren in the building of St. Paul's Cathedral. On the churchyard wall is a poignant plaque to Sgt. Pilot Bruce Hancock, who died heroically in the last war.

At the next junction you will be turning right, signposted to Little Barrington.

You may care to call in at the Fox Inn opposite this junction. It still has a skittle alley and is prettily situated by a river bridge built with funds provided by Thomas Strong, one of the same local craftsmen who had a hand in the construction of St. Paul's Cathedral. Little Barrington feels wonderfully remote. It is built around a hollow from which was excavated the stone used to build the surrounding houses. Watercress was once cultivated here. On the far side is an old water pump and the former Post Office, reputed to be the smallest in England, housed in the old smithy, with its creeper around the door, and mullioned windows, echoing the romance of its surroundings.

Burford

Continue past the green, rising up from the valley to join the A40 where you will turn left towards Oxford and Burford.

After crossing the Gloucestershire / Oxfordshire border, you will soon come to the main Burford roundabout. You will be returning later to visit the lovely town centre of Burford, but for the time being,

Follow the A40 straight towards Oxford. After a mile or so, take the first road on the left, signposted towards Widford (single track road), and then at the bottom of the hill turn right to Widford and Swinbrook.

The solitary Widford Church will appear on a rise amongst the meadows of the River Windrush.

Turn left at the crossroads into Swinbrook.

Here you can enjoy a scene that could not be anywhere else but rural England. The Swan Inn is delightfully situated by a stone bridge over the Windrush; next door is an old mill; and a lob away is a cricket pitch perfectly drawn for lazy summer afternoons and tankards of ale. In front, sheep graze on gentle slopes. The Romantic Road continues into the heart of the village, which with its stream-cleft green is set in "the lyrical, soft beauty of the world".

This description is taken from a book called "Hons and Rebels", the account of her early life by Jessica Mitford, one of the Mitford girls who were brought up here in the early part of the twentieth century. Raised in an aristocratic family of some eccentricity, Jessica herself became involved in radical left-wing politics, ran away to the Republican cause in the Spanish Civil War and settled in the USA. Her sister Unity created something of a scandal by her involvement with Hitler and the Nazis. Deborah married the Duke of Devonshire, Diana married Sir Oswald Mosley, leader of the British Fascist Party and Nancy became a noted novelist. Her version of a Cotswold childhood is recorded in "The Pursuit of Love" – romance of a unique variety.

Unity and Nancy are buried side-by-side just beyond the entrance to Swinbrook Church. Inside is the coat of arms of the Redesdale family (the Mitfords' father was the second Lord Redesdale) and the pews were donated by him following a successful bet on the Grand National. Swinbrook was the home of another eminent family, the Fettiplaces, whose local importance is clear from this couplet:

"The Tracys, the Lacys and the Fettiplaces
Own all the woods, the parks and places."

In the church six members of the family are unusually commemorated in two tiers, reclining on their sides and elbows in the costumes of their time, gazing longingly outside rather than up to heaven. Nearby is a romantic dedication to one of the clan – Edmund Fettiplace:

"Whose native myldnes towards great and small
Whose faith and love to friends, wife, children, all
In life and death made him beloved and deer
To God and meen and even famouse heer.

Blessed in soule, in bodie, goods and name
In plentieous plants by a most vertuous dame
Who with his heire as to his worth still debter
Built him this toomb, but in her heart a better."

Some 300 yards past the church, take the first road on the left. It is unmarked and leads across undulating fields to the village of Fulbrook, from where you travel the short distance into one of the most famous and romantic of Cotswold towns – Burford.

You enter at the bottom of the village by crossing a fine medieval bridge dating to 1322. It spans the Windrush next to the Weaver's Cottages and a charming mill with sculptured hedges. If time allows you to explore Burford on foot, there is a well signposted car park to the left of the main street. Here is a long sloping street of houses all in local stone and topped in local slate. There is a wonderful intermingling of buildings and dimensions, harking back to the days when Burford was an important stop on the London – Cheltenham coaching route, as well as the Midlands – South Coast run. As in times gone by, there is no shortage of hotels, inns and teahouses, as well as shops selling antiques and gifts.

Burford's great coaching days are vividly related in Edith Brill's book, "Old Cotswold", and can be seen in the old Tudor market house, the Tolsey Museum, which is easily identifiable by its large round clock projecting out over the High Street. On the more romantic note, Charles II stayed at the Bull Hotel with his colourful mistress, Nell Gwynn, during the races at nearby Burford Down. Indeed, their son was created Earl of Burford.

Lechlade

The Romantic Road passes between the lime trees at the top of the High Street and continues across the roundabout towards Lechlade and the Cotswold Wildlife Park.

Follow this road, the A361, for approximately 3¹/₂ miles ignoring all turnings until you see one on the left, marked Filkins, which you should take.

On entering the village you will see Filkins Hall on the left, opposite Cotswold Woollen Weavers. This is a working woollen mill, one of the few remaining, and uses only pure Cotswold wool. Here is what remains of the heart of the Cotswolds, for it was on the wool trade that Cotswold prosperity was built. In the Middle Ages local wool was the most sought after in Europe; and many villages owe their distinctive character to the bequest of merchants who made their fortunes from the wool trade. So this mill represents an entire epoch and continues to produce soft, romantic wools. Note the Bridal Door to the Barn as you enter!

If romance has come to signify, in part, a love of a disappearing way of life, then the life of George Swinford, a former centenarian resident of Filkins who recorded the events of his life in "Jubilee Boy" was truly romantic. Here is an unadorned account of the hard life of a stonemason, born in Filkins in 1887 and who spent the whole of his life here. Joys were few; and he does not regret the passing of the hard life. He regrets only that people have lost the facility of deriving enjoyment from small, innocent pleasures. He recalls playing marbles in front of the Bull and Lamb Inns; the excitement of visiting Lechlade Fair; his part in helping to build Filkins Hall. He worked for William Morris's pupil Gimson; and indeed he remembers seeing William Morris himself "driving along the road from Kencot across the fields in his high carriage with his wife and two daughters. When we heard his horse clip-clopping, we boys ran to close the gate and stood waiting nearby. When he got there he would raise his whip and shout "You young rascals again!" but he always threw us a penny for opening the gate."

From the Cotswold Woollen Weavers, you proceed right into Filkins. Follow the road past the Lamb Inn and the village church to rejoin the A361, where you turn left for the two miles into Lechlade. Here the rivers Leach and Coln meet the Thames, and the Thames and Severn Canal begins.

WILLIAM MORRIS AND KELMSCOTT – THE ROMANCE OF REVIVAL

Not far from Filkins, in the direction of Lechlade, is the village of Kelmscott. William Morris, craftsman, poet and visionary, lived here in Kelmscott Manor for the last twenty years of his life and is buried in the local churchyard. He described Kelmscott as "heaven on earth". In the middle of the village is a memorial cottage with a fine stone carving of Morris reclining philosophically under a tree. The Morris Memorial Hall, designed by his pupil, Gimson, was opened by George Bernard Shaw. Morris's name is well known for his contributions to English culture and to the movements in which he was involved. He was associated with the artists of the Pre-Raphaelite Brotherhood, who were fired with enthusiasm for the ideals of the Middle Ages. Morris was also a force in the revival of traditional handicrafts manifested in the Arts and Crafts Movement – indeed his recognisable style and influence in fabric and wallpaper is still felt.

The following extract taken from Morris's "Inscription for an Old Bed", seems to sum up his love for his Cotswold home.

"The wind's on the wold
And the night is a-cold
And the Thames runs chill
Twixt mead and hill
But kind and dear
Is the old house here."

Kelmscott Manor

The Market Square in Lechlade is attractive and so are the streets that run off it – Burford Street, High Street and St. John's Street. There are two fine bridges here too – the 18th century Ha'Penny Bridge and St. John's Bridge that dates back to 1228. But the romance of the town is in the vicinity of the church, one of the finest wool churches in the Cotswolds. In 1815 the poet Shelley made the journey from Windsor by boat in the company of the writer Thomas Love Peacock. He spent the night in

the neighbouring New Inn; but as the sun went down he was inspired to write "Stanzas in a Summer Evening Churchyard", from which the following extract is taken:

Thou too, Aerial pile! Whose pinnacles
Point from one shrine like pyramids of fire,
Obeyest in silence their sweet solemn spells
Clothing in hues of heaven thy dim and distant spire
Around whose lessening and invisible height
Gather among the stars the clouds of night."

A plaque by the church, along "Shelley's Walk", marks the spot where inspiration struck.

From Lechlade you initially travel along the A417 in the direction of Cirencester. On reaching Fairford, turn right into the High Street.

Fairford

Take time to visit St. Mary's, in whose church some of the most beautiful stained glass in England transmutes sunlight into a temple of colour. The church itself is almost entirely 15th century and was built by a prosperous Cirencester wool merchant. The glass, made by, it is thought, the Flanders craftsman Barnard Flower, with the help of his English colleagues, is original and has survived 500 years of vicissitude. The windows, the most complete examples of medieval glass in England, illustrate biblical scenes, starting with the temptation of Eve, continuing with the story of Christ, and ending with eternal damnation.

The Lady Chapel, in the north east corner of the church, is particularly worthy of your attention – here are portrayed the marriage of Joseph and Mary and the birth of Jesus Christ. Beneath these scenes are the tombs of the Thame family. John, the principal benefactor of the church, lies in effigy next to his wife, whom he loved dearly and who died bearing their fourth child.

A less romantic aspect of marital bliss is to be found among the carved benches beneath the choir stalls in the sanctuary – the last is of a wife "batting" (without much restraint) her errant husband! The Englishman's legendary love for animals finds expression here too – as you leave the church you will see the last resting place of a much beloved church cat, Tiddles, buried outside the church door. And opposite the church gates, a romantic police station in Cotswold stone, built in the days when the police shared premises with the magistrates' and petty sessions' court. John Keble, leader of the Oxford Movement, was born here in 1792.

THE BIRTHPLACE OF A GREAT COMPOSER

Down Ampney, near Fairford, was the birthplace of Vaughan Williams, the great English composer. His father, the local vicar, is commemorated with the resurrection scene in the church and the village itself is remembered in the tune "Down Ampney" that Vaughan Williams wrote for the hymn "Come down O love divine". You traverse a pretty graveyard to reach the church, which stands next to a handsome 15th century manor house.

From St. Mary's, continue the few yards to the end of the High Street opposite the entrance to Fairford Park and turn left into Mill Lane. After crossing the River Coln, you will arrive at a junction. Turn right and follow the signs for Coln St. Aldwyns.

Coln St. Aldwyns

Coln St. Aldwyns is a delightful village and is made up of sturdy Cotswold stone cottages. A particular welcome can be found in the charming New Inn. From the Inn with its fine coaching yard, The Romantic Road rises to the top of the main street by the wonderfully old-fashioned Coln Stores and sets off in the direction of Bibury.

Half a mile beyond Coln St. Aldwyns, take the first road on the left to Bibury (straight on points to Aldsworth and Burford).

As we approach Bibury, turn left on to the B4425, which will take you through the village.

Bibury

Bibury was described by William Morris as "the most beautiful village in England". It certainly has a very particular charm, with the shallow, crystal Coln bubbling by the roadside; and many delightful cottages and houses, the most beloved of which make up Arlington Row, a line of exceptionally pretty 17th century cottages sitting between a bank and rushy meadows. Stand on the little footbridge nearby and drink in the beauty of them and of the whole place. At the other end of the village is Arlington Mill Museum and Gallery, where there are several displays pertaining to Cotswold life and culture.

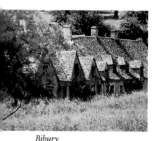

The Romantic Road

This area has more than its fair share of literary connections and the writer J. Arthur Gibbs lived at the end of the 19th century in the nearby village of Ablington. In his book, "A Cotswold Village", he attempted to record the simple annals of a quiet, old-fashioned Gloucestershire hamlet. The author does himself an injustice, for although he records much that is fascinating of the old ways, he does so with some passion and lyrical power. "Darting straight up stream on the wings of the soft south wind comes a kingfisher clothed in priceless jewellery, sparkling in the sun: sapphire and amethyst on his bright blue back, rubies on his ruddy breast, and diamonds round his princely neck. Monarch he is of silvery stream and pretty tyrant of the silvery fish".

From Bibury, your next stop along The Romantic Road is Cirencester, ancient Roman town and capital of the Cotswolds. Continue along the B4425.

Bibury

En route you will pass Barnsley Park, a fine baroque house with a "pepperpot" lodge, on the right hand side. Barnsley village is famous for its Barnsley House Gardens. The creation of Rosemary Verey, these are open to the public. The gardens are on your left beyond the "Village Inn".

To visit Cirencester, go straight ahead at the roundabout on the outskirts of the town, following signs for the town centre. Go straight ahead again at the traffic lights and then turn right into South Way, still following signs for the town centre. The road winds round to join the High Street, where you will turn left into the market place. Cirencester, in its heyday known as Corinium Dobunnorum and the second most important town of Roman Britain, was the point of convergence of three major roads – the Ermin Way, the Fosse Way and Akeman Street. There are many delightful sights to treasure in this bustling market town: the great parish church with its three-storey porch, once the town hall; Coxwell Street's unspoiled charm; a Roman amphitheatre; Cecily Hill leading to the splendour of Earl Bathurst's park. If you have time, visit the Corinium Museum.

Cirencester

To leave Cirencester from here, continue through the traffic lights by the church, along Castle Street and then follow the road round into Sheep Street. Now follow signs for the ring road and pick up signs for Stroud along the A419.

From Cirencester, take the A419 towards Stroud. Approximately 3 ½ miles out of Cirencester, look out for the small signpost on the right for Sapperton.

Take this turn and you are once again in the heart of the Cotswold countryside. Missing out Sapperton village, the road skirts the pretty green with its interesting examples of topiary, and then plunges down to the Daneway Inn.

Just by the pub, take the narrow road that climbs up to the left towards Bisley.

Through lonely wooded valleys, you will eventually come to a main road just outside the attractive village of Bisley, one of the few places in the area where the ancient tradition of well-dressing is maintained.

Cross this road carefully and go down a narrow street until you meet the main street where you should turn right. Follow this amongst the stone cottages until you see a small Post Office and grocery stores on the right. Take the road on the left, directly opposite the store.

You will pass by the "lock-up" on the right and the splendid 17th century Bear Inn, supported by its fine Jacobean pillars.

This is a friendly hostelry and its open fireplace makes it as snug as any pub in the Cotswolds. In the pub, you may even hear tell of the popular legend of the Bisley Boy who became Queen Elizabeth of England! Sources will relate how the young princess stayed the night at the old Butler's Court beside the churchyard, where she inexplicably and suddenly died. Her guardians were fearful of the King's wrath and searched the village for a red-headed girl, who could take her place. Alas, to no avail and they substituted a boy of the same age who consequently had to play the role of the princess and then later the Queen. This accounts for the reason why Queen Elizabeth never married and was such a powerful ruler – or so the story goes . . .

Continuing past the Bear for approximately half a mile, you take the second turning on the right, signposted to Camp and Birdlip.

This is an old drover's route called the Calf Way.

At the next T junction, turn left again, signposted to Camp and Birdlip.

Just after The Camp, you turn left at a somewhat unromantic electricity station, towards Sheepscombe. At the crossroads with the B4070, go straight across towards Sheepscombe, followed shortly by a right hand fork to Sheepscombe Village.

You now dive down into the "Peaceful Valley", which rates as one of the most beautiful in the Cotswolds. Sheepscombe has a further claim to fame as one of the villages associated with the late Laurie Lee. His book, "Cider with Rosie", (published in North America as "Edge of Day"), about his childhood in the early years of the 20th century has already become a pastoral classic. Here is the romance of a way of life not long distant in time, but which was the continuation of hundreds of years of unchanging custom which has now all but disappeared. It is not merely a collection of observations, but also the story of the approach of manhood and the awareness of the possibilities of romance (". . . for me, the grass grew longer, and more sorrowful, and the trees were surfaced like flesh, and girls were no longer to be treated lightly but were creatures of commanding sadness, and all journeys through the valley were now made alone"). It is, too, the story of his mother ("I absorbed from birth, as now I know, the whole earth through her jaunty spirit"), of local characters ("Granny Trill and Granny Wallon were traditional ancients of a kind we won't see today, the last of that dignity of grandmothers to whom age was its own embellishment"). Perhaps more than any other, Laurie Lee succeeded in capturing the romance of the Cotswolds in all its beautiful complexity.

After passing the Village Hall, The Romantic Road rises up steeply from the valley to go by the local pub, the Butcher's Arms, and to follow the winding road towards Painswick.

The soaring spire of Painswick church provides a distinctive landmark.

Following signs to Painswick, The Romantic Road will bring you to the junction with the A46 where you should turn left.

It is just a short distance into Painswick. To visit the town, pass down the narrow High Street, and park in the car park beyond the Church. The entrance is on the left in Stamages Lane. Painswick is known as the "Queen of the Cotswolds". It is a little gem of a town of silver grey stone houses, worthy of exploration on foot. By the time you arrive at this point on your Romantic journey, you will probably wish to enjoy afternoon tea at one of the town's delightful tea rooms. The town is famed for its 99 Yew trees growing in St. Mary's churchyard *(pictured left)*. Local legend has it that the devil prevents the 100th from growing. Note also the 17th and 18th century table tombs. One of the attractions of Painswick is the famous Rococo Garden. A unique restoration of an 18th century garden from the brief Rococo period, it is set in a hidden valley affording magnificent views.

Painswick Rococo Garden

From Painswick retrace your steps through the town, travelling north along the A46 towards Cheltenham.

As you journey you will pass on the left a large pub called the Royal William. Continue straight on here and follow this road as it spirals in a long descent towards the vale below.

The escarpment rises steeply above you to the right, covered with a cool forest of ancient beech.

Before long, a signpost marked Prinknash Abbey will appear on the left.

Prinknash Abbey

England, and particularly Gloucestershire, was at one time quite overrun with monasteries, until their dissolution in the 16th century. This Benedictine monastery, however, was built in 1939 to house the monks who had formerly lived on Caldey Island. The site had for centuries been the property of the Abbots of Gloucester and the old house can still be seen on the hillside. The writer, Horace Walpole, visited the old house in 1774: "It stands on a glorious but impracticable hill in the midst of a little forest of beech, and commanding Elysium". The new monastery boasts a pottery, bird park, chapel and café, all of which are open to the public throughout the year.

The road continues its descent past Cooper's Hill.

This is the scene of one of the more bizarre Cotswold traditions. Every Spring Bank Holiday Monday in May locals gather in a line at the top of the cliff-like hill, then at a given signal speed off in hot pursuit of the "cheese" that is despatched down the hill. The first to reach the bottom receives a genuine whole Double Gloucester. This is no mean achievement, all the more so if accomplished without injury. The origins of this curious ceremony are obscure but it is thought that there may be associations with fertility and spring, with the cheese symbolic of the Sun. The cheese rolling is still an annual event of considerable popularity.

The road curls downwards and straightens
up towards the roundabout at Brockworth.
The road to Cheltenham carries straight across.

Beyond the roundabout, the road flattens out
to take you through Shurdington and back
towards Cheltenham.

Devil's Chimney, Leckhampton Hill

On the right you will pass the entrance to an Elizabethan country house, now the Greenway Hotel, with its fine formal gardens. As you approach Cheltenham, the full length of Leckhampton Hill, its former quarries distinguishable by its exposed outcrops of golden limestone, can be seen above you to the right. Not easily visible at this distance is the intriguing Devil's Chimney, which is associated with the following legend:

The Greenway Hotel

Gloucestershire was noted, as we have seen, for its churches and abbeys, much to the displeasure of the Devil. In his anger and bitterness, he would hide on this ledge to extract boulders with his trident, which he would then lob onto the pilgrims passing below. All to no avail, however, for the boulders came piling down on the Devil himself, driving him underground. The stone chimney is a symbol of his simmering anger.

As you return to Cheltenham, one more piece of verse from another of the area's great poets, Ivor Gurney, will serve to accompany you into our Regency spa town and leave you, it is hoped, in good heart.

"The gardens grow as freshly
On Cotswold's green and white;
The grey-stoned cottage colours
Are lovely to the sight,
As we were glad for dreams there,
Slept deep at home at night."

Attractions along The Romantic Road

A ROAD FOR TODAY

CHELTENHAM

Cheltenham Art Gallery & Museum
Clarence Street,
Cheltenham GL50 3JT
☎ 01242 237431
Free Admission
Open all Year

Pittville Pump Room
Pittville Park,
Cheltenham GL52 3JE
☎ 01242 523852
Open All Year

WINCHCOMBE

Sudeley Castle & Gardens
Winchcombe GL54 5JD
☎ 01242 602308

Hailes Abbey
Winchcombe GL54 5PB
☎ 01242 602398

TODDINGTON

Gloucestershire/Warwickshire Steam Railway
The Railway Station,
Toddington GL54 5DT
☎ 01242 621405

A ROAD FOR TOMORROW

YANWORTH

Chedworth Roman Villa
Yanworth GL54 3LJ
☎ 01242 890256

NORTHLEACH

Cotswold Heritage Centre
Fosseway, Northleach
GL54 3JH
☎ 01451 860715

Keith Harding's World of Mechanical Music
High Street, Northleach
GL54 3ET
☎ 01451 860181
Open All Year

BURFORD

The Tolsey Museum
126 High Street, Burford
OX18 4SE
☎ 01993 823647

Cotswold Wildlife Park
Burford OX18 4JW
☎ 01993 823006
Open All Year

STANWAY

Stanway House
Stanway GL54 5PQ
☎ 01386 584469

SNOWSHILL

Snowshill Manor
Snowshill, Broadway
WR12 7JU
☎ 01386 852410

BROADWAY

Broadway Tower & Country Park
Broadway, off A44
☎ 01386 852390

CHIPPING CAMPDEN

Hidcote Manor Garden
Hidcote Bartrim
GL55 6LR
☎ 01386 438333

Kiftsgate Court Gardens
Nr Mickleton,
off B4081/B4632
☎ 01386 438777

Woolstaplers Hall Museum
High Street,
Chipping Campden
☎ 01386 840289

LECHLADE

Kelmscott Manor
Kelmscott, Nr Lechlade
GL7 3HJ
☎ 01367 252486

FILKINS

Cotswold Woollen Weavers
Filkins, Nr Lechlade GL7 3JJ
☎ 01367 860491
Open All Year

BIBURY

Arlington Mill Museum & Art Gallery
Bibury GL7 5NL
☎ 01285 740368
Open All Year

Bibury Trout Farm
Bibury GL7 5NL
☎ 01285 740215
Open All Year

BARNSLEY

Barnsley House Garden
Barnsley House, Barnsley,
Nr Cirencester GL7 5EE
☎ 01285 740281
Open All Year

BLOCKLEY

Mill Dene Garden
Blockley GL56 9HU
☎ 01386 700457

MORETON-IN-MARSH

Batsford Park Arboretum
Moreton-in-Marsh, on A44
☎ 01608 650722

Sezincote
Moreton-in-Marsh
GL56 9AW
(Contact by writing only)

LOWER SLAUGHTER

The Old Mill Shop & Museum
Mill Lane, Lower Slaughter
GL54 2HX
☎ 01451 820052

CIRENCESTER

Corinium Museum
Park Street, Cirencester
GL7 2BX
☎ 01285 655611
Open All Year

PAINSWICK

Painswick Rococo Garden
The Stables, Painswick
GL6 6TH
☎ 01452 813204

CRANHAM

Prinknash Abbey & Visitor Centre
Cranham GL4 8EX
☎ 01452 812066
Open All Year

Prinknash Bird Park
Prinknash Abbey,
Cranham GL4 8EX
☎ 01452 812727
Open All Year

Churches

A ROAD FOR TODAY

Cheltenham
St. Mary's Parish Church

Winchcombe
St. Peter's

Stanway
St. Peter's

Stanton
St. Michael & All Angels

Chipping Campden
St. James'

Broad Campden
St. Michael's

Blockley
St. Peter & St. Paul

Moreton-in-Marsh
St. David's

Stow-on-the-Wold
St. Edward's

Naunton
St. Andrew's

A ROAD FOR TOMORROW

Northleach
St. Peter & St. Paul

Widford
St. Oswald's

Swinbrook Church

Burford
John the Baptist

Lechlade
St. Lawrence

Fairford
St. Mary's

Bibury
St. Mary's

Cirencester
St. John Baptist
Parish Church

Bisley
All Saints

Sheepscombe
St. John's

Painswick
St. Mary's

Prinknash Abbey